GRAPHIC SCIENCE

THE SOLID TRUTH ABOUT STATES OF MATTER

WITH **MAX AXIOM** SUPER SCIENTIST

Agnieszka Biskup

illustrated by Cynthia Martin and Barbara Schulz

www.raintreepublishers.co.uk
Visit our website to find out
more information about
Raintree books.

To order:
☎ Phone +44 (0) 1865 888066
🖹 Fax +44 (0) 1865 314091
🖳 Visit www.raintreepublishers.co.uk

Raintree is an imprint of Capstone Global Library Limited, a company incorporated in England and
Wales having its registered office at 7 Pilgrim Street, London EC4V 6LB
Registered company number: 6695882

"Raintree" is a registered trademark of Pearson Education Limited, under licence to Capstone Global
Library Limited

Text © Capstone Press 2008
First published by Capstone Press in 2008
First published in hardback in the United Kingdom by Capstone Global Library in 2010
The moral rights of the proprietor have been asserted.

ISBN 978 1 406 21452 9 (hardback)
14 13 12 11 10

British Library Cataloguing in Publication Data
Biskup, Agnieszka.
States of matter. -- (Graphic science)
530.4-dc22
A full catalogue record for this book is available from the British Library.

Art Director and Designer: Bob Lentz
Cover Artist: Tod Smith and Krista Ward
Colourist: Michael Kelleher
UK Editor: Diyan Leake
UK Production: Alison Parsons
Originated by Capstone Global Library
Printed and bound in China by South China Printing Company Limited

Acknowledgements
The publisher would like to thank the following for permission to reproduce copyright material:
BigStockPhoto.com p. 11 (Joeshmo); Shutterstock pp. 7 (Paul Paladin), 15 (Julien Grondin)

CONTENTS

As he cleans up his work space, Super Scientist Max Axiom begins to think about the nature of matter.

It's amazing how many things we have around us. Computers, TVs, books, magazines, furniture, you name it!

But what's even more amazing is that it's all made of the same stuff.

Everything you see — every chair, book, and speck of dust — is made of matter.

But it's not just objects. Everything alive — every tree, plant, and animal on earth — is made of matter too.

And your car has a lot more mass than you do. But at 87 kilograms, or 192 pounds, you have more mass than me.

That's right. Let's explore what matter is made of.

57 kg
125 lbs

87 kg
192 lbs

 MASS AND WEIGHT

We usually think of mass and weight as being the same thing, but they really aren't. Weight is the measure of the pull of earth's gravity on an object. On the moon, an object would weigh only one-sixth of what it would weigh on earth. For example, a 5.4-kilogram (12-pound) bowling ball would only weigh 1 kilogram (2 pounds) on the moon. Although the weights would be different, the mass would be the same.

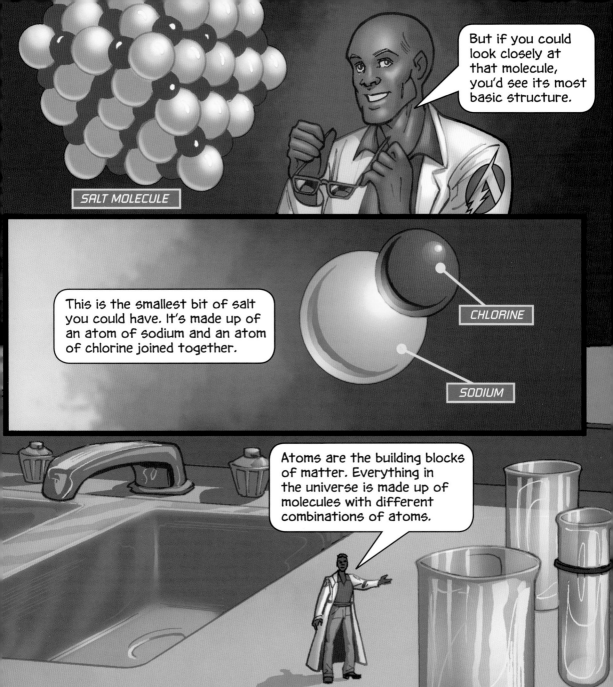

SALT MOLECULE

But if you could look closely at that molecule, you'd see its most basic structure.

This is the smallest bit of salt you could have. It's made up of an atom of sodium and an atom of chlorine joined together.

CHLORINE

SODIUM

Atoms are the building blocks of matter. Everything in the universe is made up of molecules with different combinations of atoms.

PARTS OF THE ATOM

Atoms can be broken down into even smaller building blocks called neutrons, protons, and electrons. The number of protons an atom has defines what type of atom it is. Hydrogen has one proton, helium has two, and carbon has six.

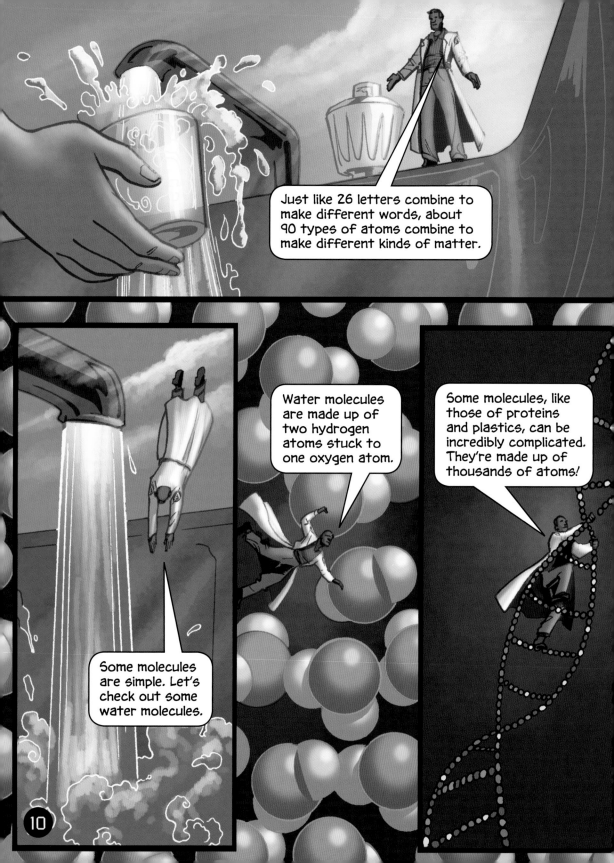

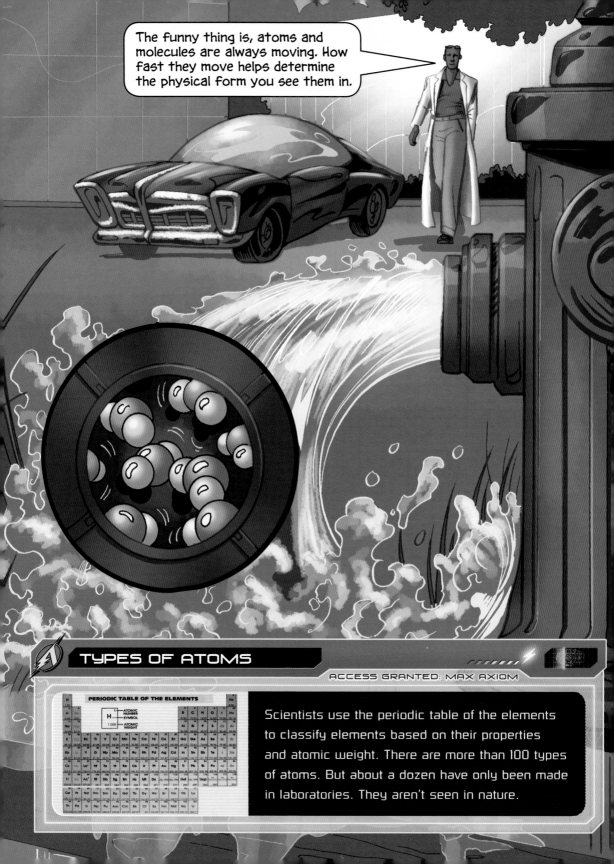

The funny thing is, atoms and molecules are always moving. How fast they move helps determine the physical form you see them in.

TYPES OF ATOMS

ACCESS GRANTED: MAX AXIOM

Scientists use the periodic table of the elements to classify elements based on their properties and atomic weight. There are more than 100 types of atoms. But about a dozen have only been made in laboratories. They aren't seen in nature.

The physical form of matter depends on the energy of the atoms and molecules.

Matter can exist in three states. It can be a solid, a liquid, or a gas.

For example, water can exist as solid ice, as liquid water, and as a gas, such as steam.

SOLID

LIQUID

GAS

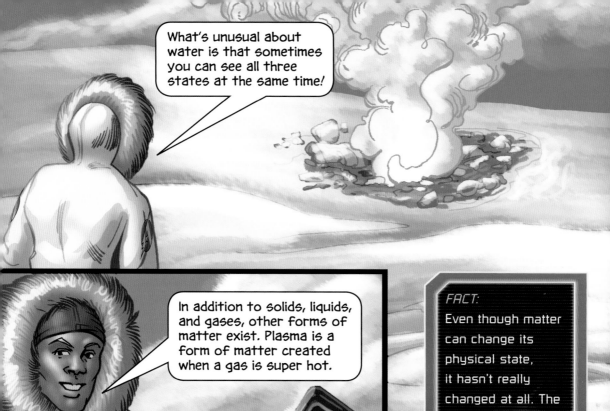

What's unusual about water is that sometimes you can see all three states at the same time!

In addition to solids, liquids, and gases, other forms of matter exist. Plasma is a form of matter created when a gas is super hot.

It's so hot that the electrons are torn free from the atoms, and the plasma is able to conduct electricity. Lightning is made of plasma.

FACT:
Even though matter can change its physical state, it hasn't really changed at all. The molecules that make it up are still exactly the same whether it's a solid, liquid, or gas. Water is still water, and will behave like water, whether it's ice, liquid, or steam.

The sun and stars are also made of plasma.

Plasma may be the most common form of matter in the universe, but it's rare on earth.

Let's take a closer look at the three states of matter we normally see.

Solids have a definite shape that isn't easy to change. Rocks, ice, and hunks of iron are all solids.

Changing a solid's shape is difficult. Its molecules are linked together and are usually packed very closely.

The molecules in a solid barely move at all. They just vibrate in place.

ICE CRYSTAL

In a crystal of ice, the atoms stick together in an organized pattern. They're locked in place and only twist or turn a little.

14

When you heat a solid, the molecules start moving around more. As you increase the heat, the organized pattern of the molecules starts breaking apart.

The molecules are still close together, but they're not as tightly packed. They can slip and slide over each other. They change states from a solid to a flowing liquid by melting.

MELTING ROCKS

ACCESS GRANTED: MAX AXIOM

Lava, anyone? Even rocks melt at high enough temperatures. Some rocks can melt at the relatively low temperature of 704 to 816 degrees Celsius, or 1,300 to 1,500 degrees Fahrenheit.

If you continue heating a liquid, the molecules start moving very fast. Eventually, they fly apart and the liquid turns into a gas.

In a gas, molecules are far apart. In fact, a gas is made up of mostly empty space.

That's why we can walk through a gas like air and not feel anything.

At the boiling point, the molecules in a liquid get enough heat energy to completely break free from each other. Bubbles of gas form in the liquid.

In a pot of boiling water, the bubbles you see are made of water gas, or water vapour. They rise to the top and burst, forming a cloud of steam.

Different substances have different boiling points. Some oils boil at 204 degrees Celsius, or 400 degrees Fahrenheit.

And iron boils at around 2,871 degrees Celsius, or 5,200 degrees Fahrenheit.

And you can boil a diamond too! But a liquid's boiling point can vary with changes in pressure. Let's see how!

VOLUME

ACCESS GRANTED: MAX AXIOM

The volume of a solid always stays the same. So does the volume of a liquid. But where a solid keeps it shape, a liquid will flow to settle at the bottom of a container, whatever its shape. Gas, however, has no set shape or volume of its own. It will expand to fill any space available.

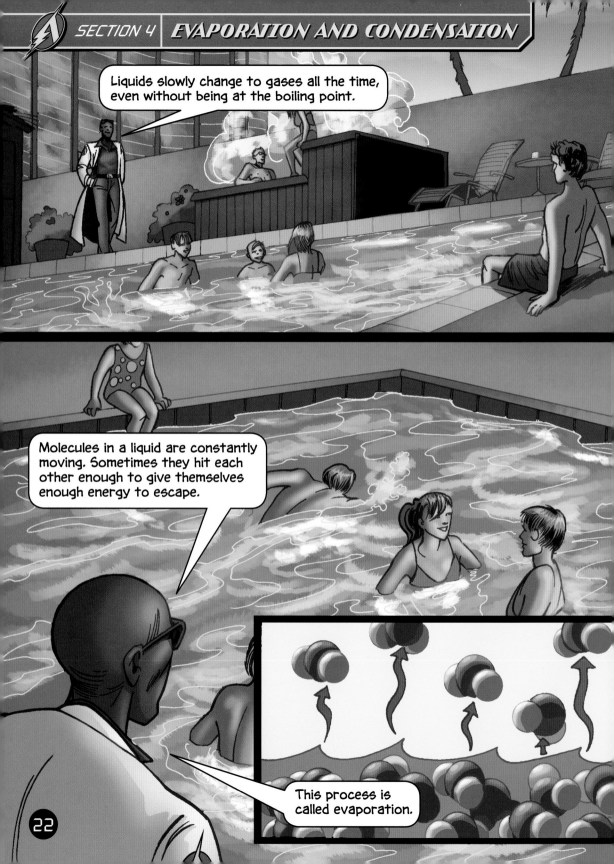

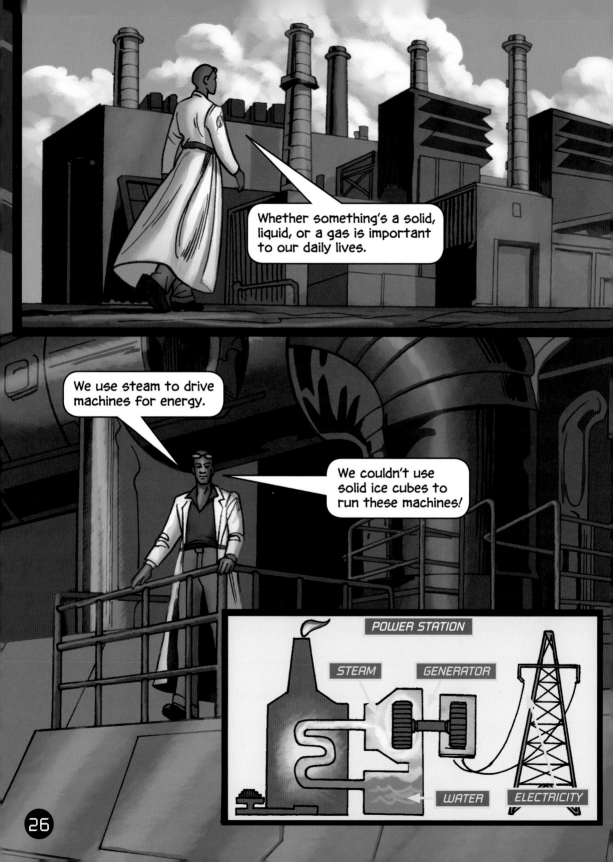

MORE ABOUT
STATES OF MATTER

More than 2,000 years ago, the Greek philosopher Leucippus came up with the idea that there was only one type of matter. He guessed that if you could cut matter up over and over again, you'd eventually get to a piece of matter you couldn't divide any further. His student Democritus called these tiny indivisible pieces of matter "atoms".

Atoms are made up of even smaller particles called protons, neutrons, and electrons. But protons and neutrons are made up of even tinier particles called quarks. Some scientists think quarks are as small as things get. Others scientsts aren't so sure. They believe quarks themselves may be made up of even smaller things called strings.

In the past few years, scientists have created two new forms of matter. These atoms are Bose-Einstein condensates and fermionic condensates. These exotic forms of matter can exist only under very special and extreme conditions in a laboratory.

It may sound like science fiction, but antimatter does exist. Scientists have created antimatter using huge, high-tech machines. Antimatter particles are like mirror images of the particles that make up our normal world. There are antimatter protons and electrons, for example, called antiprotons and positrons. A particle and its antiparticle are the same, except that they have opposite electrical charges. But if they ever meet up, watch out! The particles destroy each other and disappear in a burst of energy.

A gas can be cooled down to make it into a liquid or solid. Oxygen is normally a gas, but at minus 183 degrees Celsius, or 297 degrees Fahrenheit, it becomes liquid. Oxygen will become a solid at minus 219 degrees Celsius, or minus 362 degrees Fahrenheit.

 Pure substances have defined freezing points. But you can change the freezing point of a pure substance by adding an impurity, such as salt, sugar, or alcohol. For example, when salt is added to water, the freezing point of water drops by a few degrees. That's why people put salt on icy streets and roads in the winter. The salt makes it less likely the streets will ice over.

MORE ABOUT

SUPER SCIENTIST

Real name: Maxwell Axiom
Height: 1.86 m (6 ft 1 in.)
Weight: 87 kg (13 st. 10 lb.)
Eyes: Brown   **Hair:** None

Super capabilities: Super intelligence; able to shrink to the size of an atom; sunglasses give X-ray vision; lab coat allows for travel through time and space.

Origin: Since birth, Max Axiom seemed destined for greatness. His mother, a marine biologist, taught her son about the mysteries of the sea. His father, a nuclear physicist and volunteer park warden, showed Max the wonders of the earth and sky.

One day, while Max was hiking in the hills, a megacharged lightning bolt struck him with blinding fury. When he awoke, he discovered a new-found energy and set out to learn as much about science as possible. He travelled the globe studying every aspect of the subject. Then he was ready to share his knowledge and new identity with the world. He had become Max Axiom, Super Scientist.

GLOSSARY

atmosphere mixture of gases that surrounds the earth

atom element in its smallest form

condensation the act of turning from a gas into a liquid

electron tiny particle in an atom that travels around the nucleus

evaporation the act of turning from a liquid to a gas

gravity a force that pulls objects together. Gravity pulls objects down toward the centre of the earth and the moon.

matter anything that has weight and takes up space

molecule smallest part of an element that can exist and still keep the characteristics of the element

neutron one of the very small parts in an atom's nucleus

particle tiny piece of something

proton one of the very small parts in an atom's nucleus

sublimation the act of turning from a solid to a gas

vapour a gas made from something that is usually a liquid or solid at normal temperatures

volume amount of space taken up by an object

FIND OUT MORE

Books

Changing Materials (Material World series), Robert Snedden (Heinemann Library, 2007)

Changing Materials (Understanding Science series), Penny Johnson (Schofield and Sims, 2007)

Changing States: Solids, Liquids, and Gases (Do It Yourself series), Bill Hurd (Heinemann Library, 2009)

Experiments with Water (Do It Yourself series), Chris Oxlade (Heinemann Library, 2009)

Website

www.bbc.co.uk/schools/ks2bitesize
Click on "Science" and then "Materials" for activities and quizzes on topics such as "Changing state", "Solids, liquids and gases", "Reversible and irreversible changes" and "Solids and liquids"